Original title:
Moonlight in the Mulch

Copyright © 2025 Creative Arts Management OÜ
All rights reserved.

Author: Nolan Kingsley
ISBN HARDBACK: 978-1-80567-373-6
ISBN PAPERBACK: 978-1-80567-672-0

The Night's Breath on Vines and Blooms

In the garden where critters lurk,
The shadows dance, giving a smirk.
Grapes giggle as they wiggle free,
Whispering secrets to a bumblebee.

With carrots in capes, they stand so proud,
Telling tales to the clouds that crowd.
The zucchini wears glasses, quite astute,
Pondering life, munching on fruit.

Hushed Moments Beneath the Evening Stars

A tomato in a top hat, what a sight,
Claiming the seat of the stars at night.
As cucumbers tumble, laughter ensues,
While lettuce debates the best dancing shoes.

Celery kids snap and giggle so loud,
Spinning their dreams like a cheeky crowd.
Under the gaze of sleepy-eyed owls,
They share stories of pots and gardening fowls.

Dim Light Among the Fertile Ground

In twilight glow, the carrots take flight,
With radishes rehearsing for a delight.
They tap dance on soil as worms watch with cheer,
Wondering how they hold joy oh so dear.

A potato rolls by, full of glee,
Chasing the moon like it's a bumblebee.
Spud in the lead, they form a line,
A veggie parade, everything feels fine.

Night's Glow on Summer's Harvest

Cabbages chuckle, wrapped up so tight,
As radishes waltz under the starlight.
Pumpkins with puns that float in the air,
Joking with squash, oh what a rare flair!

A corn stalk stands tall, sporting a crown,
Bragging that it will never come down.
In the soft hush, as darkness bestows,
Veggies giggle on while the night lightly glows.

Dappled Light on Welsh Clay

Under a starry umbrella,
Worms wear tiny hats,
They dance in the shadows,
As crickets tip their spats.

Frogs croak delightful tunes,
While snails race on their shells,
The hedgehogs all applaud,
In peculiar, prickly swells.

Beetles juggle acorns,
With laughs that echo bright,
As moonbeams waltz around,
In this soft, silly night.

The rabbits flash their grins,
As they play hopscotch in dirt,
Adding to the laughter,
In their muddy little spurt.

Celestial Soil Underfoot

In the garden of the bizarre,
Gnomes sip lemonade,
Trading stories 'neath the stars,
In this peculiar glade.

The flowers wear goofy hats,
While roots start to giggle,
The pots join in the fun,
With every clunk and wiggle.

Dancing moles sneak a peek,
With twinkles in their eyes,
They pop up for a joke,
And dive back with surprise!

Beneath the glowing stars,
Frolics never cease,
In the soil of laughter,
A world of crazy peace.

Glow of the Night-Scarred Earth

In the twilight's silly gaze,
Crickets hold a fair,
With shadows dancing lightly,
And laughter in the air.

Mice draw doodles in the moss,
With twigs as their brush,
Under twirling beams of light,
They paint without a rush.

The owls offer advice,
With wisdom quite absurd,
"Don't wear socks with flip-flops,
It's truly quite unheard!"

Fireflies start a conga line,
Their buzz a happy song,
As the night-tinged earth glows,
And we all dance along.

Glistening Paths Through the Undergrowth

Wander paths of shimmered dreams,
Where squirrels tell tall tales,
In thickets filled with laughter,
And raccoons wear their veils.

The mushrooms round as jesters,
Invite all to their show,
With giggles pulling vines,
As the willow trees bend low.

Ladybugs in a parade,
On a ladybird spree,
With tiny flags of joy,
In their insect jubilee.

Through the glistening undergrowth,
Each critter plays its part,
In this whimsical ballet,
That brings the night to heart.

Gentle Hues on the Forest Floor

A glow in the garden, what a sight,
The worms wear top hats, oh what a night.
The chipmunks are dancing, move with flair,
While squirrels juggle acorns, without a care.

We'll toast to the critters, in this grand show,
With a party of leaves, let's give it a go.
The raccoons are laughing, what a parade,
As shadows do waltz, in a secret glade.

A soft breeze whispers, tickles the ground,
Frogs croak in rhythm, quite the sound.
The shadows are silly, they leap and play,
Under a blanket of stars, they sway.

So let's raise a cheer, for this merry crew,
In the foliage glimmers, there's much to do.
With giggles and shimmies, the night wears a crown,
As the fancy of nature takes over the town.

Illumination in the Earth's Embrace

A twinkle from dirt, how absurdly bright,
The gophers are plotting some wild midnight flight.
With the glow just right, not a moment too soon,
They plan to dig tunnels, like moles on the moon.

Giggles from roots, that tickles the toes,
While the daisies take bets on who grows the most.
A butterfly's disco, in the fern-filled den,
The night brings a party—let joy not end!

The ants parade by with tiny tuxedoes,
Hors d'oeuvres of crumbs for the fanciest shows.
Laughing till dawn, while the plants stand tall,
With a shimmer of humor, they conquer it all.

So let's join the fun in this earthy delight,
With laughter that bubbles, like sparks in the night.
Amidst all this madness, let's dance a bit more,
As the dirt gives a chuckle, right to its core.

Echoes of Night in the Soil's Breath

Sounds of the dark, a comical tune,
The earthworms are crooning beneath the full moon.
To the rhythm of roots, life's whimsical play,
The beetles take bets on who'll win this ballet.

With giggles and squeaks, the night creatures cheer,
While shadows play tag, without any fear.
The slugs in their shells are the slow-motion stars,
As fireflies blink like little teen cars.

The owls share gossip, oh what a scene,
With tales quite ridiculous, if you know what I mean.
A raccoon in pajamas, struts with great pride,
While the grasses all giggle, they simply can't hide.

The violets all hum, in the sweet evening air,
As laughter erupts, from the critters laid bare.
In the hush of the night, where the antics unfold,
A story of folly is quietly told.

The Quiet Pulse of Starry Night

Beneath twinkling skies, in the hush of the dark,
The rabbits in tuxes are ready to spark.
With a hop and a skip, they take to the floor,
For a ballet of bunnies, with leaps to explore.

While the ferns giggle softly, they join in the fun,
Shooting starlit glances, they twirl one by one.
The night holds its breath, as laughter takes flight,
With the creatures of whimsy, from dusk until light.

The bushes are shaking, what a sight to behold,
As sleepy-eyed hedgehogs share stories retold.
With giggles and wiggles, the whole forest knows,
That a party of critters is where the fun grows.

So let's revel in joy, till the break of first dawn,
In this wild, leafy dance, where all worries are gone.
From the sounds of the soil to the laughs in the air,
Under the blanket of stars, we all share the care.

Enchanted Hours with Night's Glow

In the garden, gnomes take flight,
They twirl and spin in the soft twilight.
With their hats askew, they chase the mice,
Laughing loud, oh, isn't that nice?

Fireflies join in the jubilant cheer,
Doing the cha-cha, oh so near.
While worms compete in a limbo spree,
Who knew the soil held such glee?

Twinkling Hues Among the Harvest

Carrots wear wigs made of green,
Potatoes form a dancing machine.
Pumpkins roll out in a boo-boo bash,
Their orange laughter a riotous splash.

Zucchini twirls with saucy zest,
They all shout, "We're the garden's best!"
And in the back, with a silly grin,
A squash named Bob declares, "Let's begin!"

The Glow of Twilight's Tapestry

Under the stars, the tomatoes sing,
While peas play tag and the radishes swing.
As the garlic claps, the onions sigh,
With every joke, they reach for the sky.

Chives are the comedians, telling good tales,
And leeks bring the laughs, as the night exhales.
They gather round for a merry old show,
In this patch of fun, there's always a glow.

Shadows Dancing on Fertile Ground

The soil whispers secrets; it's quite unkempt,
With shadows doing tango, all night exempt.
Glistening beetles with two left feet,
A dance party's brewing—it's hard to beat!

Nearby, a cabbage wears glasses anew,
Pretending to read the funny reviews.
But as laughter echoes through the dark, you know,
This garden knows how to put on a show!

Night Whispers Among the Blossoms

In the garden, shadows prance,
Crickets sing in a strange dance.
Rabbits hop beneath the moon,
Wearing hats, they hum a tune.

The flowers giggle, stems do sway,
As bugs debate who'll win today.
A snail moves slow, with pompous flair,
Claiming this path as his own fair share.

The daisies gossip, stir the air,
A butterfly conducts with care.
Bees appear in tuxedos tight,
Buzzing softly about their night.

In this mulch, beneath a song,
Everything feels just right, not wrong.
With every chuckle, every cheer,
The garden's laughter fills the sphere.

Celestial Guidance on Lush Terrain

In grassy fields where daisies wink,
Lizards don their shades and think.
A wise old owl gives jokes at night,
While fireflies flicker, just for light.

Worms wear monocles, quite aloof,
Debating whether to raise the roof.
Silly voices in the air,
Gossiping 'bout the sun's last glare.

A squirrel wearing sneakers flies,
Chasing dreams across the skies.
While beetles dance, their tiny feet,
Creating rhythms oh so sweet.

Can you hear the laughter loud?
Nature thrives, both strong and proud.
In this adventure, join the fun,
Under stars, until the day is done.

Silent Lullabies in the Garden

The night sings soft, a lullaby,
As a hedgehog waves hello, oh my!
Beneath the bushes, whispers grow,
To the stars, the flowers show.

The toads croak out, a comic play,
While sleepy blossoms drift away.
Butterflies wear shades of mint,
While snoring bunnies seem to glint.

Don't wake the worms, they're snoozing tight,
In their cozy homes, wrapped up tight.
The moon's a jester, casting beams,
Joking with the garden's dreams.

In this haven, laughter blooms,
Nature's theater holds no gloom.
Join the fun, embrace the night,
With giggles growing, pure delight.

Traces of Light Where Shadows Linger

In the shadows where giggles hide,
The critters crawl in a funny tide.
A frog tells tales of grand old times,
While stars twinkle, dressing in rhymes.

The soil whispers secrets sweet,
As moles break dance with tiny feet.
Fireflies flash, a lively parade,
Lighting up every leafy glade.

An ant in a cape, off on a quest,
Searching for crumbs, he's feeling blessed.
He accidentally bumps his head,
And finds a mushroom bed instead!

Laughter sprouts in every nook,
Nature's pages, a comic book.
So join the fun, where shadows play,
In this garden, night turns to day.

The Garden's Secret Hours

Rabbits wear shades under the stars,
Chasing shadows of well-fed jars.
Gnomes in a huddle, swapping their tales,
While the snail brigade slowly unveils.

Worms whisper secrets, while ivy snores,
A ladybug dances on leaf-covered floors.
The daisies giggle, their petals aflutter,
As toads read poetry over the gutter.

Crickets chirp jokes in rhythmic delight,
And the old oak tree joins in the fight.
Butterflies trade their nightgown gowns,
As the garden spins in fourteen clowns.

When morning approaches, they don their disguise,
With sleepy apologies and half-opened eyes.
The sun stretches wide, it's time to depart,
Leaving the secrets to rest in the heart.

Echoes of Light in the Growth

Fireflies flicker in a comical dance,
While cabbages plot to take a chance.
A beetle complains about shoes that are tight,
Stepping on zucchinis with all of its might.

Petunias continue their gossip and glee,
"Did you see what the radish did? Oh, me!"
Daffodils nod, with a flick of their flair,
While bumblebees twirl through the crisp, cool air.

The garden is giggling, a clandestine joke,
As mushrooms tease what the pumpkins bespoke.
Even the roots are shaking with laughter,
Over tales of a cat who ran faster.

In the shadows, the echoes softly chuckle,
While the vegetables prepare for their shuffle.
As sunlight breaks in with a yawn and a sigh,
They promise to meet again, oh my!

Secrets Buried in Soft Darkness

In the nighttime's warmth, the secrets abide,
A cat in a cloak brews tea for a ride.
While the marigolds keep their wisdom in rhyme,
And rosemary sings to the rhythm of time.

A hedge of ivy wears eccentric hats,
Discussing the mischief of all the bats.
The carrots are jesters, their tops in a tangle,
Playing charades with the light from a dangle.

The glow-worms giggle at stories well-told,
Of how the old fence was once brave and bold.
A chorus of ants lays down the beat,
As the thyme twirls round without missing a beat.

But come the dawn, their laughter fades fast,
Hiding their fun until shadows are cast.
When darkness returns with a wink and a nod,
The garden awakens to gala and applaud.

Elysian Gardens By Night

Daisies in dresses out on the lawn,
Twirl to the hum of a soft, light yawn.
Roses are painting their petals with zest,
While shadows waltz in a whimsical quest.

A troupe of toads form a band by the gate,
Playing tunes that are strangely quite late.
They croak out a symphony, bass and then high,
As the crickets compose their nocturnal lullaby.

Sunflowers share tales of their day in the sun,
While the moonbeams laugh, it's all just for fun.
Pairs of owls argue on who's the best sage,
Scripted in riddle, a very wise page.

And when sunrise beckons, a break in their night,
The garden will rest till the next moon's light.
With secrets to share under skies filled with cheer,
They'll wait for return of the night, full of queer!

Twilight Dances Among the Ferns

In the garden, shadows prance,
Frogs in tuxedos break their stance.
Worms wear hats and strut with flair,
While crickets giggle in the air.

A comet's tail trails over leaves,
As ants hold court with grand reprieves.
The night is young, let's cause a stir,
With grasshoppers buzzing, 'What's the fur?'

Celestial Rays on the Humble Bed

The phlox are dressed in shimmering dress,
While daisies gossip, 'Who's the best?'
A row of tulips lines the street,
In funky patterns, oh, so neat.

Gnomes toss marbles, playing a game,
With ladybugs who stake their claim.
A snail on cruise, taking his time,
Laughed out loud, 'Hey, life's sublime!'

Luminous Secrets of the Hidden Earth

The beetles gather for a feast,
Sipping nectar with a twist of yeast.
The roots are tangled, making some noise,
While moles are plotting their playful poise.

Badgers perform a waltz in the dirt,
With earthworms grooving in their shirt.
Each secret shared with laughter and cheer,
As stars peek down, 'What's happening here?'

Beneath the Canopy, Light Unfolds

Squirrels debate how to steal the show,
While owls roll eyes at the ruckus below.
Leaves spin stories on the cool breeze,
As toads play hide-and-seek with ease.

The nightingale sings the funkiest tune,
With frogs as backup, under the moon.
Branches sway to the rhythm of cheer,
Saying, 'What a hoot, let's dance, my dear!'

Light Unfolds

The glimmering stars share a wink or two,
As the shadows groove, making their debut.
The evening's mischief is quite the sight,
Under a cloak of gleeful twilight.

Dandelions burst forth, a fluffy parade,
With giggling seeds, in the cool shade.
The earthworms cheer, 'Now that was grand!'
While the starlight shimmers, hand in hand.

Radiance Through the Rooted Dream

Beneath the stars, the carrots dance,
They twirl and spin, given half a chance.
A cabbage sings a silly tune,
While beets play tag beneath the moon.

The radishes bust out some bold moves,
Challenging potatoes to prove their grooves.
Tomatoes giggle, blush a bright red,
As worms in jackets shimmy, half dead.

The lettuce tosses its fluffy head,
Any veggie here can join the spread.
In this garden jamboree each night,
The roots are reveling, pure delight.

So if you peek through the garden gate,
Be quiet now, don't tempt your fate.
Lest a runny squash throws beans your way,
You might just join their wild ballet!

Silvery Veils on Fertile Ground

A beet so bold in shiny attire,
Claims it's the best, a garden flyer.
"Come watch my glow, I've got the looks,
I'm the selfie king among these cooks!"

The pumpkins roll, their laughter bright,
Making shadows dance in the pale light.
With whispered secrets, the onions plot,
To pull a prank on the carrots' spot.

The chickens cluck, as if they know,
That greens do gossip, a steady flow.
Spinach winks, in jest declares,
"I dare anyone to match my pairs!"

So when you stroll past the garden patch,
Beware the jibes, they're hard to catch.
You might just find, among the whirls,
A cabbage caper that surely twirls!

Nightfall's Embrace in Green Depths

In the shadiest corner, peas conspire,
Whispering dreams of a veggie choir.
Leeks take notes as they scribble songs,
While underground, the mushrooms dance along.

The herbs all join in with fragrant cheer,
Mint plays the flute, basil's near.
Each leaf tips its hat, takes a bow,
Together they make a raucous vow.

A hedge of broccoli flexes its might,
Declares it perfect for a veggie fight.
Yet just then, a radish rolls by,
And suddenly, there's laughter in the sky.

So roam through the greens, embrace the fun,
Where veggies play games 'til day is done.
For in this patch, so lively and bright,
The humor blooms in the glow of night!

The Glow That Nurtures

In the garden bed, where gophers peek,
The veggies share tales, both mild and cheek.
"Did you see that root, a daring sight?
It tried to dance but lost the fight!"

Kale cracks jokes, sporting leafy flair,
While radishes giggle, flipping their hair.
Zucchini flexes, saying, "Look at me!
The squash is dropping lines, oh, can't you see?"

A butterfly floats, joining the show,
Painting the air in whimsical flow.
The beans burst out laughing, their pods a-grin,
While carrots race round to join in the din.

So if you visit this lively plot,
Take a few minutes, connect the dots.
For in this garden, beneath the night,
Laughter and roots share the same delight!

Light's Touch on Nature's Canvas

A glow creeps in with bubbling cheer,
The garden dances, oh so near.
Worms in tuxedos sway to the beat,
While crickets tap on tiny feet.

The daisies wear their best nightgowns,
As shadows play like little clowns.
A tomato blushes, feeling fine,
Under the stars, he sips some wine.

Fireflies twinkle, stars in disguise,
Telling tall tales with flickering eyes.
Each leaf a canvas, stories unfold,
Of muddy mischief and laughter bold.

So watch the night, embrace the glee,
In this wacky world, come dance with me.
The soil is alive, it's clear to see,
Nature's stage is where we're free!

Ethereal Glow in the Garden's Heart

A sparkly dust on petals bright,
Goblins prance in the pale moonlight.
Radishes giggle in whispered tones,
As onions laugh, they have no bones.

Pumpkins argue who's the most round,
While spinach breaks into joyful sound.
A leaf with glasses reads a book,
In the glow of a friendly nook.

Ants throw a party, fancy and neat,
Served by beetles, such a treat!
Beneath the stars, they hop and swing,
In this silliness, all hearts take wing.

The night unfolds its playful yarn,
Where laughter echoes through the barn.
So tiptoe close, join the delight,
In nature's jest, we'll dance all night!

The Night's Palette in Greenery Fields

In the meadow, colors collide,
As flowers giggle, they won't hide.
Cucumbers tango with cheeky glee,
Under the sky, wild and free.

Beans in bowties slide and glide,
While turnips joke, filled with pride.
Carrots sport their best green hats,
Snickering softly at silly sprats.

Fragrant herbs start their own band,
Playing tunes across the land.
Tomatoes belt a ballad sweet,
As night's adventure stirs to greet.

So join the fun, don't think too long,
In the fields, we all belong.
With nature's brush, let's paint the cheer,
Under the stars, let's disappear!

Hidden Luminescence in the Patch

Underneath the curly vines,
Lurks a world of witty lines.
Zucchinis sport their shiny coats,
While critters plan their little votes.

A cabbage whispers jokes so wise,
As peas roll eyes and share surprise.
The radishes giggle from the earth,
Celebrating their leafy birth.

Nighttime brings the silliest game,
Beetles prancing, what's their name?
The patch is alive, with crafty cheer,
Cackling softly, it's all quite clear.

So come and share a lighthearted jest,
In this garden, it's all the best.
Hidden wonders, at every squeeze,
Laughter echoes through the leaves!

Shimmering Fields Beneath the Firmament

Underneath the sparkling glow,
The garden gnomes throw quite a show.
They dance and prance in silver light,
While rabbits giggle at their delight.

The daisies twirl and share a laugh,
As crickets take their funny path.
A sunflower cracks a witty joke,
And all the plants begin to poke.

The beetles wear their shiny hats,
As squirrels play tunes on old tin vats.
The night grows wild with quirk and cheer,
While slumbering worms dream with no fear.

So raise a toast, you silly blooms,
To nights that dance in thrilling zooms.
In fields so bright with laughter's might,
We twirl in joy till morning light.

The Whisper of the Night's Depth

In whispers soft, the shadows sway,
The owls crack jokes, they love to play.
A mischievous mouse with a cap so grand,
Plans funny pranks on the sleeping band.

The stars above snicker in glee,
As fireflies waltz with utmost spree.
A cat plays tricks with a flick of a tail,
While snorting badgers tell a tall tale.

The moon beams down a glimmering wink,
As flowers giggle and softly blink.
The hedgehogs roll in a fit of glee,
Creating chaos—oh, what a spree!

With nature's quirks lighting the dark,
Each night unfolds a new, funny spark.
In this playful world that lifts our mood,
We join the dance, oh how it's good!

Glowing Dreams Among the Foliage

Among the leaves, a lantern glows,
Where silly berries tell their prose.
A wiggly worm dressed in bright green,
Snickers at things he's never seen.

Toadstools hold a comedy night,
As frogs hop in, ready to bite.
Each croak and ribbit, a punchline tight,
Underneath the stars, what a sight!

A timid deer begins to prance,
With squirrels coaching her in dance.
Laughter echoes through the trees,
Even the moss can't help but tease.

So gather 'round, you brave little sprout,
Let's share a giggle—oh, there's no doubt!
In this glowing grove so bright and wild,
Nature's humor never goes mild.

Twilight's Embrace on Wooden Trails

On forest paths where shadows play,
The twilight greets the end of day.
A chipmunk juggles acorns with flair,
While bunnies snicker without a care.

Old trees lean close, they start to chat,
About the silly things they've spat.
A raccoon rolls in leaves, so bold,
With stories of mischief, oh, so old.

The night gives birth to giggles bright,
As owls perform their stand-up right.
A wise old fox in a tiny vest,
Cracks jokes that put the critters to rest.

So wander here on nature's track,
Where laughter fills the night with no slack.
Each furry friend and leafy mate,
Embrace the fun—it's never late!

The Spell of the Darkened Garden

In the garden, shadows dance,
Bugs wear top hats, take a chance.
Flowers giggle, roots do sway,
Nighttime parties, what a play!

Raccoons waltzing, quite the sight,
Silly squirrels join in the light.
Crickets sing with goofy cheer,
Who knew guests would disappear?

A gnome throws up a wild shake,
Beneath the stars, they all partake.
Laughing petals in a spin,
What a night, let fun begin!

When dawn arrives, they'll snooze away,
Till night returns for round of play.
In the garden's silly fright,
Wonders hide from morning light.

Ethereal Gleams Among the Upturned Leaves

Glowing orbs in dirty soil,
Twirling bravely, they uncoil.
Worms in tuxedos crawl around,
A fashion show beneath the ground!

Frogs recite their ribbit songs,
While snails look on and hum along.
Mice hold hands and wait their turn,
For moonlit magic, they all yearn.

Underneath the leafy dome,
Creatures frolic far from home.
Each twinkling spark brings the cheer,
Who knew nature had a beer?

As dawn breaks, the laughter fades,
Still, echoes dance in leafy glades.
Waiting for another night,
When upturned leaves will laugh in light.

Echoes of Light in the Wild's Embrace

Wiggly shadows beg to play,
In the glow of cool ballet.
Owl in glasses takes his flight,
Tutors all on how to bite!

Beetles wearing shades of green,
Tap-dance out to make a scene.
Silly whispers fill the air,
Chortles bounce from here to there.

Starlit critters tell their tales,
While fireflies juggle snails.
What a crowd of giggles found,
Nature's jesters, world-renowned!

But when the sun comes shining through,
The mischief hides—it's nothing new.
Hidden smirks on fading tracks,
Await the night for silly acts.

Dreaming Underneath the Celestial Veil

Under twinkling dreams awake,
Laughter rises, bonds they make.
Goblins hide in the grass tall,
Just waiting for a midnight call!

Glistening chairs of rustic wood,
Host the quirkiest of the brood.
Round they spin, then take a dive,
In this whimsy, all alive!

Fables bounce on breezy nights,
Stories told with funny sights.
Sneaky hedgehogs roll in glee,
Seeking snacks from each old tree.

When sleepy heads return to rest,
They dream of jokes and silly quests.
Till darkness brings the giggles back,
Under stars, they fill the lack.

Ethereal Gleam on the Ground

A shimmer spills across the yard,
As critters dance and live large.
The gnomes are laughing at the toads,
While daisies gossip in funny codes.

The hedgehog wears a jaunty hat,
While worms compose a silly chat.
A raccoon juggles fallen fruit,
And in the dark, the ants dispute.

Oh, what a sight in the night air,
With wiggly roots that do not care.
The daisies spin in spiraled fun,
And giggle till the day is done.

As shadows stretch and squirrels play,
Beneath the stars, they laugh away.
Each twinkling wink, a joke untold,
In nature's theater, dreams unfold.

Secrets of the Starlit Patch

In the garden, whispers tease,
As fireflies buzz and sway with ease.
A beetle talks in riddles grand,
While daisies sway, hand in hand.

The carrots wiggle, feeling spry,
While the radishes all just sigh.
The moon pulls pranks on all around,
And laughter echoes from the ground.

A ladybug slips on a leaf,
Clumsy critters bring relief.
With every giggle, shadows hop,
In the glow, the fun won't stop.

Oh, secrets lie beneath the stars,
As laughter floats on silvery bars.
With every rustle, another joke,
In the patch where mischief woke.

Silhouettes Beneath Lunar Glow

Silly shadows take their form,
Beneath the night, they twist and swarm.
The squirrels dance a goofy jig,
While frogs audition for the big.

The grasshoppers boast of their height,
As crickets chirp, prepared to fight.
Each time a breeze blows past their way,
They tumble down and giggle, hey!

Dirt piles whisper funny tales,
Of butterflies with tiny sails.
The roots beneath, in laughter's bliss,
Form friendships spawned from quirky risks.

So let the night bring out the cheer,
With every chuckle bringing near.
In nature's play, we find our place,
Amongst the sprouting jokes we chase.

Celestial Reflections in the Dirt

In the patch, the roots are wise,
They wink and glow with funny eyes.
The stones are gabbing, oh so bright,
As shadows play in pure delight.

The snails debate who's the fastest,
While a turtle boasts, he's the lastest.
Each beetle tells a fanciful tale,
And every chuckle lights the trail.

The moon hangs low, a thoughtless host,
As crickets plot a midnight roast.
A worm provides an unexpected twist,
Ensuring no fun is ever missed.

With every giggle, seeds take flight,
As dirt and laughter mix at night.
In this spectacle of glee,
Nature's fun is wild and free.

A Song for the Midnight Bloom

In the garden where shadows play,
The flowers dance and sway all day.
The crickets sing a silly song,
While worms wiggle and strut along.

A cabbage wore a shiny hat,
Pretending it was a fancy cat.
The daisies laugh and tease the weeds,
As raindrops drip like funny beads.

A rogue raccoon came for a feast,
He juggled berries like a beast.
With every hop, a playful shout,
He flings the compost, watch it sprout!

So let's embrace this silly night,
With giggles blooming, pure delight.
The garden glows with jests so grand,
In this funny, leafy wonderland.

Glimmers of the Nightshade

There's a glow beneath the starlit hue,
Where nightshade dances, oh so true.
The shadows wiggle, twirl and spin,
While toads in tuxedos loudly grin.

The carrots hold a poker game,
Betting veggies for some fame.
A startled radish shouts, "Oh dear!"
While onions cheer, "Let's start the cheer!"

With every chuckle, sprouts awake,
As fireflies join the silly quake.
The laughter spreads, it's quite the show,
As peas start rolling, oh what a flow!

The thrill of nightshade's playful birth,
Is a celebration, joy and mirth.
In every nook, a joke's unfurled,
Creating smiles in the garden world.

Radiance Above the Ripe Mulch

Beneath the stars, a glow so bright,
A humble rhyme brings pure delight.
The squash are grinning, what a sight,
As critters gather for the night.

With giggles hidden in the dirt,
The earthworms wear the finest shirt.
Potatoes dance with zest and flair,
While beetles boogie everywhere!

The radishes spin in sheer delight,
As laughter echoes through the night.
With every root, a tale untold,
Of whimsy, mischief, brave and bold.

So join the fun, don't sit aloof,
In this garden, raise the roof!
With playful spirits, let's rejoice,
As every plant sings with a voice!

Whispered Tales of the Evening Soil

In the evening's cozy nest,
The daisies gossip, doing their best.
With whispers soft, they share their dreams,
While silvery moonbeams wink and beam.

The ants hold court, they pass the time,
Discussing earth with rhythmic rhyme.
A fat toad croaks, as if to say,
"Join the party, come and play!"

The tucking petals close their eyes,
While snails wear hats and eat the pies.
A riddle from a curious vine,
"Who's the jester? I'll be divine!"

With every whisper, a chuckle spreads,
As nature giggles and nods its head.
So gather round, my friends, let's share,
This funny soil, beyond compare!

Chasing Light Through Garden Shadows

In the garden when darkness falls,
The plants start to sprout their quirky calls.
A gnome trips over a daisy's grace,
While sneaky squirrels dance in a race.

A flashlight flickers, a beetle squeaks,
As shadows play, the humor peaks.
The flowers giggle with blossom pride,
While rabbits hop like they've got a ride.

With each turn of the night's gentle page,
The crickets play tunes, creating a stage.
A garden of whimsy, laughter unfurls,
In this world where night capers whirl.

So here's to the antics, the silly sights,
Of creatures and critters in silent nights.
They dance and they frolic, beneath the stars,
Every shadow a giggle among the jars.

Luminescence Among the Weeds

The weeds sway gently like wild hair,
As fireflies gather, plotting a flare.
In the thicket, a hedgehog blinks,
Confused by the glow; he hardly thinks.

A garden hose twists, like a snake in fright,
While rabbits perform in the glow of the night.
They hop and they jump, without a care,
As the weeds sigh loudly, 'This just isn't fair!'

The moon peeks down, a silver grin,
Witnessing jokes of the garden kin.
A snail makes a dash, calls it a race,
Yet still takes an hour, with abundant grace!

With laughter echoing through the green,
Nature's a stage, with a comical scene.
From blossoms to bugs, they all share a laugh,
In a world where the weeds chart their own path.

Starlit Serenade in the Underbrush

Under the stars, the night takes a swing,
As frogs in the pond begin to sing.
Their chorus a melody, silly yet grand,
While a raccoon strums with a twig in hand.

A wandering owl hoots with delight,
As shadows prance in their playful flight.
The bushes chuckle, the vines intertwine,
In this concert of chaos where all things align.

A mouse with a phobia of moonbeams bright,
Dances in circles, lost in his plight.
While ants parade with a flower bouquet,
Saying, "We rule the garden; hip-hip-hooray!"

So join the jubilee, in underbrush bright,
With critters and chuckles in the soft light.
Each critter a star in this zany fest,
Where laughter erupts and nature's the best.

Mysteries of the Twilight Earth

When twilight camouflages the space behind,
That's when the gnomes start to unwind.
They tumble and roll through the dampened grass,
In a chase for the light, oh what a task!

A buzz from a bee lured too close to the sun,
Stumbles and fumbles, thinking it's fun.
A garden of chaos, where silliness thrives,
Creatures unite, keeping laughter alive.

A worm in a top hat, declares a grand ball,
He flicks his tail, and the beetles enthrall.
Inquiring minds seek the night's hidden clues,
Wondering what in the garden renews.

So let's twirl with the fireflies, giggles in store,
For the secrets of night, who could ask for more?
In the patch of the earth, where jokes come to play,
Let's dance in the twilight, till the break of day.

Serenity Amidst the Darkened Green

A frog sings loudly to the night,
His croak a tune, a comical sight.
An owl hoots back with wise appeal,
While the crickets dance with zestful zeal.

The timid mouse peeks from the grass,
His little heart races, hopes he'll pass.
But a cheeky bug lands right on his nose,
He sneezes and jumps, oh how the fun goes!

In the shadowed grove, where laughter rings,
A raccoon sneaks in with shiny things.
He steals a snack, then drops a treat,
A hilariously clumsy nighttime feat.

But amidst the giggles and the delight,
All nature whispers, "What a wild night!"
And in this oddball dance, we embrace,
The silliness wrapped in foliage's grace.

Sheltered Dreams Beneath a Silver Glow

A bushy-tailed squirrel does a flip,
While leaves below prepare to rip.
He lands with grace but looks quite shocked,
As the acorn bounces off and rocks.

A snail, with swagger, glides about,
His pace so slow, he draws a pout.
Yet laughter blooms with every inch,
He's the poet of the night, without a flinch.

The shadows blend with a playful grin,
As shadows hide the night's chagrin.
Each beetle chuckles under the sky,
In this wild world, they easily fly.

With every chuckle, the branch may sway,
As twilight turns to playful play.
Here dreams shelter in a cozy, warm place,
Where every critter shares a joyful face.

Whispers of the Celestial Soil

The garden gnome watches in delight,
As the ants parade in the pale twilight.
He cheers them on with a crooked smile,
As they march together, mile after mile.

A shy little worm gets in the groove,
With a squiggle and shimmy that can't help but move.
The daisies sway, joining the dance,
In this wacky procession, all take a chance.

A thistle starts to tickle the night,
As the fireflies join in, glowing bright.
They twirl and swirl, in a twinkling jest,
Making every critter feel quite blessed!

But what's this I hear, a raucous sound?
A hedgehog tumbles right off the ground!
With laughter echoing through the soil,
Such joy abounds, alive and royal.

Silver Shadows on Earth

A bumblebee buzzes, up for a game,
While the daisies shout, "Join in the fame!"
The grasshoppers leap with a silly flair,
Making quite the ruckus, up in the air.

A frog wears glasses, cool as can be,
His hipster vibe is plain to see.
While a fancy snail performs a slow jig,
Their comical moves are always big.

But there's a skunk that joins the fun,
He prances in, and we all run!
Yet just in time, he snorts a grin,
And we collapse in laughter, no fear within.

As stars giggle in their distant heights,
The fun continues through the whimsical nights.
Each shadow dances beneath the sky,
In this merry gathering, oh me, oh my!

Night's Caress on Shade and Soil

Under stars, the critters play,
A wiggly worm leads the ballet.
With tomatoes dressed in evening gowns,
The cucumber wears a crown of towns.

A sneaky raccoon steals a bite,
While fireflies dance, oh what a sight!
The carrots giggle, carrots murmur,
As shadows leap, the garden stirs.

The radishes in wine glasses cheer,
"Another party, let's not fear!"
The lettuce winks, "We'll have a blast!"
Beneath the sky, the night goes fast.

In the darkness, life's a jest,
Join the fun, it's for the best!
With every leaf that sways and tilts,
A secret world, with laughter built.

The Gentle Edge of Darkness

When crickets chirp and shadows creep,
A garden gnome starts counting sheep.
The pumpkins roll on grassy knolls,
While mischievous squirrels plot their goals.

The moon peeks out from cloud's embrace,
Paints the weeds with a smoky lace.
A patch of dirt that sparkles bright,
Turns the weeds to stars of night!

"Who left those shoes?" a flower quips,
As dandelions share their tips.
The tulips laugh, their heads held high,
In this strange land, the odd things fly.

With every rustle, every sound,
A squirrel's acrobatics abound!
So raise your glass, a toast to play,
At the garden's edge, we'll find our way.

Radiant Secrets of the Garden Floor

A chipmunk's stash beneath the tree,
Hides giggles whispered, "Look at me!"
The daisies blush, their petals wide,
"Let's host a party, come inside!"

With tiny toasts of dew and dirt,
The crawling bugs, all dressed in spurt.
The roses joke, "We're feeling fine!"
Beneath the stars, we sip on brine.

A beet sneezes, sprays a friend,
Laughing, they plot to do it again.
The shadows dance, a comic spree,
In the land where veggies roam free.

The gardener snores, oblivious bliss,
As ladybugs share a dreamy kiss.
So raise a leaf, and shout hooray,
In this garden, let's jest away!

Afterglow in the Whispering Leaves

As night descends, the leaves do sway,
With rustling secrets of the day.
The herbs converse in hushed delight,
"Shh, the carrots are a bit uptight!"

The lilacs giggle at a snail's race,
While wandering stars play hide and chase.
Cucumbers giggle, "What a show!"
As mint insists, "We'll steal the glow."

The garden cat with sly intent,
Prowls on paws that barely vent.
A comedic fight 'twixt mole and gnome,
While daisies dream of far-off home.

And when the sun returns to play,
They'll spin their tales of last night's fray.
For every leaf that sways and speaks,
Lies a world of laughter, beyond the peaks.

Starlit Harmony in Nature's Cradle

In the garden, a raccoon danced,
Under twinkling lights, he pranced.
With a twirl and a skip, oh what a sight,
He thinks he's the king of the night!

Crickets chirp, a band of cheer,
While a squirrel hoards acorns near.
The moon winks down on this silly spree,
Nature's fun fair, come join the jamboree!

A hedgehog rolls, quite out of tune,
Painting shadows beneath the moon.
With each little wiggle, they strut their stuff,
In nature's ballet, the funny is tough.

So let us laugh in the nighttime glow,
Where the shadows play, and the giggles flow.
In this cradle of life, all jesters unite,
Under starlit laughter, oh, what a night!

Glimmers in the Organic Abyss

A glowworm giggles, a wink in the dark,
While a gopher tries to hit the park.
His little legs paddle, a comical race,
Digging up treasures, quite out of place.

Mice in tuxedos plot their grand heist,
Sneaking past owls who sleep without thrice.
With cheese as the prize, they plot with glee,
What a ridiculous plan, who'll take the decree?

A frog croaks loudly, quite full of charm,
Catching flies with his smirk, such a harmless harm.
Under the starlit, glimmering clatter,
They croon serenades, it's all a bit platter!

In nature's abyss, laughter abounds,
Where delight takes shape in whimsical sounds.
So join the parade, let chuckles resound,
In this glimmering realm, funny things are found!

Enchanted Beams on the Undergrowth

Beneath the beams, a rabbit slips,
With sticky paws, and wobbly hips.
He leaps for a carrot, but lands in a pot,
Such a silly prank, he's tangled in knots!

A hedgehog dines on a pie of weeds,
While snails slowly dance in their grassy beads.
All around them, the fireflies cheer,
'What a feast, what a year, let's all disappear!'

A squirrel fiddles with some sad old strings,
While frogs join in, belting tunes like kings.
Laughter rolls out like the night's own sigh,
As the stars nod their heads and join in the lie.

In the undergrowth, joy's freely spread,
With whimsical shenanigans to be led.
Beneath enchanted beams, let's play, delight,
In the quirky ballet of the funny, bright night!

Reflections of the Quiet Night

In quiet nights where shadows shimmer,
A raccoon plots, his eyes all a-glimmer.
With stealthy paws and a comical grin,
He digs for treasures—it's where he begins!

The beetles roll out, a parade on the drive,
Marching along in a bustle, alive.
They clack their shells in a rhythm so fine,
Making music on leaves, add some light wine!

A wise old owl hoots with a flair,
As the night creatures gather, all in a stare.
"What's this all about?" he asks in surprise,
"Who knew nighttime could be such a prize?"

So let's raise a toast to the night's silly lore,
Where reflections of laughter give room to explore.
In the quiet of dusk, fun takes flight,
With creatures who revel till dawn's early light!

Whispers of Lunar Soil

Beneath the beams of silver light,
The gnomes pop in for a late-night bite.
With pizza slices made of dirt,
They dance and twirl in their little skirt.

The worms wear hats, a sight to see,
Playing tag with the bumblebee.
A raccoon juggles shiny stones,
While crickets hum their silly tones.

The carrots laugh as they take a ride,
In a wheelbarrow that's way too wide.
And frogs recite their best dad jokes,
As all the bushes giggle like blokes.

The flowers sway with a cheeky grin,
As the sneaky snails try to creep in.
In this muddy fest, joy is the queen,
Where everything's funny, and nothing's mean.

Shadows Beneath the Starlit Canopy

Under a quilt of twinkling stars,
A raccoon strums on rubber guitars.
The hedgehogs hoot in harmony,
While fireflies take to the dance floor, whee!

The shadows flinch as light does beam,
Giggling squirrels join in the dream.
A cheeky mouse in a tiny hat,
Does handstands on the old straw mat.

The plants chuckle as they sway,
With roots that serve the finest clay.
A night like this, with friends galore,
What more could one silly critter ask for?

And in the quiet, laughter reigns,
A joyful chorus, life gains planes.
In this frolic, none can oppose,
The merry spirit that ever grows.

Mysteries in the Garden's Gloom

In shadows deep where secrets dwell,
The potatoes plot and weave a spell.
With swishing tails and twinkling eyes,
They scheme beneath the vast dark skies.

The beetles play hide and seek so bold,
While peas gossip stories untold.
A daffodil whispers tales of delight,
As the moon chuckles with all of its might.

A shadowy cat with a grand old grin,
Kicks up the leaves and joins in the din.
With petals twirling, they form a line,
Trust me, it's all rather divine!

And then in the gloom, a chorus takes flight,
With a funny dance that feels just right.
In the mystery, laughter is key,
Where all creatures share joy, oh so free!

Gleam Above the Earthly Tangle

The sun sets low, the stars ignite,
A crab takes the lead and starts a fight.
With tiny shoes that squeak and squeal,
He claims the turnip like a big deal.

In the tangle of green, the fun begins,
As rabbits challenge to winner spins.
A beetroot blushes, oh so shy,
As chickens cheer and lettuce flies by.

The curly tendrils twist and twine,
As garden banners puff and shine.
The night casts fun, a silly spark,
As all join in till it's getting dark.

From the gleam above, joy falls like rain,
To earth's embrace, no need to feign.
In this tangled joys, it's always clear,
That fun and laughter float right here!

Beneath the Nocturnal Canopy

Under the stars, the critters play,
Dancing and laughing, they sway.
A hedgehog with socks, quite the sight,
Stealing the show in the pale twilight.

The rabbits in top hats, they prance,
With wild carrots, they twist in a dance.
Fireflies join, a flickering crew,
Making night parties feel quite new.

A raccoon lounges, snack in paw,
Plans to build a dumpster heist, oh the law!
His friends cheer on with a joyous roar,
Plot twists ahead, oh what a score!

As shadows mingle with giggles loud,
This whimsical garden, it's truly proud.
The night can't help but join the fun,
Under the stars, the laughter's begun.

Luminous Veils Among the Roots

Glowing fungi wear hats with glee,
Poking fun at the ants sipping tea.
Worms in shades, oh how they swing,
Fashionistas in soil, they own the bling!

Beneath leafy crowns, a party's alive,
A snail in sunglasses, he's ready to jive.
He's grooving with bees on this soil dance floor,
And the bugs all cheer for a chance to encore!

Caterpillars boast of their grand designs,
Planning their flight in their nighttime lines.
But as they spin, an owl hoots loud,
"Keep it down, beauties! I'm trying to nap proud!"

With every rustle, the critters conspire,
Drawing the night into joyous choir.
Under the canopy, fun takes its root,
In a world where even grasshoppers hoot!

Night's Embrace in the Garden

In a patch where strawberries giggle and squish,
A raccoon declares, "Now let's make a wish!"
The flowers all murmur, "What's our delight?"
"We want some snacks under cover of night!"

Mice with backpacks scurry and roam,
Hitching rides on fireflies, making it home.
"Where's the cheese?" cries one little lad,
As squirrels conspire, it's quite the fad!

A disco ball spins from an old oak tree,
Spiders with glitter weave webs with glee.
Crickets keep time, a lively beat,
Inviting the blooms to bounce on their feet!

As laughter erupts from the rooty brigade,
The night bears witness to a fun escapade.
In this garden of glee, the mischief's the goal,
Where nothing feels better than dancing with soul!

Glistening Dreams in the Dark

Deep in the garden, the shadows arrive,
With daisies that giggle and jive.
An otter with glasses surveys the scene,
Sipping sweet nectar, feeling sheen!

The beetles, they gather, a conga line forms,
Wiggling in rhythm, their joy now transforms.
While the moon hangs high, a spectator bright,
Encouraging laughter to fill up the night!

Twirling amid roots, an owl takes a bow,
And the frogs are croaking, "Hey, check us now!"
With each tiny leap and enthusiastic croak,
They embody the joy of this evening's joke!

In whispers of wind, stories unfold,
Of wild little parties no one could hold.
In whimsical gardens, let all spirits play,
Where dreams sparkle bright till the end of the day!

Night's Warmth on the Earth's Skin

Underneath the blanket, snug and tight,
Worms throw a party, all through the night.
Dancing with radishes, quite the sight,
Giggling at shadows, in sheer delight.

Crickets crack jokes, while the roots sway,
Pumpkins laugh loudly, 'It's our parade!'
The soil is jiving, what a display,
Riddles and rhymes as they dance and play.

Bees wear their shades, sipping on nectar,
While tomatoes waltz, showing their vector.
The earth hums a tune, an unusual vector,
Beneath the soft stars, a wise old protector.

With each small chuckle, the night grows bright,
As the veggies share secrets and take flight.
Nature's own comedy, pure and upright,
Bringing us joy till the morning light.

The Light We Seek Beneath the Grapevine

Among the vine leaves, shadows play,
Grapes gossip softly, in disarray.
'Why are we hanging?' they often say,
'Get down from here; it's a cabaret!'

A squirrel drops by, wearing a hat,
Sipping on juice, chatting with a cat.
'You think we're wise?' the raccoon sat,
Plotting their heist, oh, imagine that!

Wobbling down, they spot a snack,
Chasing each other, no thought to lack.
Crumbs of cheese, now that's the hack,
Dinner has come on this merry track!

Through the moonlit nights, friendships grow,
As laughter echoes, high and low.
With grape-juice dreams, they steal the show,
Under the stars that happily glow.

Illuminated Paths to Hidden Fruits

Shiny paths lead, through dew-sparked leaves,
Strawberries chuckle, with silly heaves.
Corn stalks stand tall, with mischief that weaves,
Whispers of berries, the gossip that cleaves.

A rabbit hops in, wearing shoes so bright,
Giggling at carrots, in pure delight.
The roll of the dice, it's all in the night,
They toast to the moon, a shimmering sight.

The scarecrow winks, 'Oh, how do you do?'
'Join us,' says cabbage, with a smile that's true.
This veggie soirée, oh, who knew?
Leaves fall in rhythm, it's a grand debut!

When dawn approaches, the laughter will fade,
But echoes of joy will dance in the glade.
With roots in the ground, their plans will upgrade,
'Til next moonlit gathering, friendship's parade!

Sparkling Veins Beneath Earthy Skin

In the garden realm where the misfits roam,
Potatoes discuss how to find their home.
With skins made of laughter, they start to comb,
Through layers of stories, just waiting to foam.

Beetles in bowties, sipping on tea,
Whisper of dreams, 'We'll plant a spree!'
Life's too short to just roll with the spree,
Beneath the topsoil, there's joy to decree.

They scramble to dig for the truth and jest,
Finding their treasure puts them to the test.
'Let's make a smoothie!', they shout, so blessed,
Those sparkling veins, they know they're the best!

In the twilight glow, they sing songs of cheer,
With each gentle giggle, they draw everyone near.
Rooted in laughter, they're gathered here,
For in this wild garden, the fun is sincere.

Fragments of Light on Tilled Soil

In the garden, shadows play,
The worms do dance, hip-hip-hooray!
A carrot chuckles, sharing jokes,
While radishes laugh like silly folks.

A beet in shades of crimson bright,
Winks at a plan that feels just right.
With glimmers twinkling all around,
Their midnight jokes are quite profound!

The lettuce whispers, 'What a sight!'
'The moon's forgotten, hopes to write!'
A cucumber slips and starts to roll,
While peas pop out with cheeky goals.

So in this patch of humor's glow,
The soil sings as night winds blow.
With every chuckle, joy's unfurled,
As nature giggles, 'What a world!'

Starlit Paths of Nourishing Ground

In the dark, the squash do plot,
While singing songs, they dance a lot.
Tomatoes giggle, hanging tight,
Underneath the stars so bright.

The clever corn spies from afar,
'Are we the best?', it says, 'We are!'
As beans entwine and frolic free,
They toast to moon's delicious tea!

The radishes whisper nighttime tales,
As crickets join with chirpy trails.
With starlit paths through the rich earth's crust,
Every veggie laughs, it's simply a must!

And in this space of leafy cheer,
Frogs join in, they've nothing to fear.
With funny friends, together bound,
They giggle deep in nourishing ground.

Echoes of Evening in the Roots

Beneath the dirt, the laughter thrums,
As carrots bounce like little drums.
Potatoes hide with cheeks so round,
While sproutlings giggle underground.

'Whose leaf is bigger?' they debate,
As beet greens swish, feeling so great.
The radishes tease with funny pranks,
Daring the onions to join their ranks!

The squash inspires a raucous cheer,
'Embrace the dirt, cast off your fear!'
With echoes ringing through the night,
Every root united in delight.

Among the twirls of glee and jest,
The soil holds laughter at its best.
In secret, plants spin tales so cute,
As froggy friends applaud in suit.

The Night's Tender Touch in the Garden

As twilight drapes a velvet sheet,
The sprouts begin their dance so sweet.
A sunflower bows with a playful dip,
While radishes take a family trip.

'What's the punchline?' whispers a chive,
'With veggie pals, we feel so alive!'
Even the turnips have a laugh,
Counting their greens, they're on the path!

The squash jokes twist in leafy lines,
'What's growing bigger?', every vine chimes.
The night caresses each cheeky sprout,
And fosters giggles, leaving no doubt.

So in this garden, funny and free,
The plants unite for their jubilee.
With the night's tender touch around,
They frolic joyfully, earthy, and sound.

www.ingramcontent.com/pod-product-compliance
Lightning Source LLC
Chambersburg PA
CBHW071835160426
43209CB00003B/303